Special thanks to our adviser:
Susan Kesselring, M.A., Literacy Educator
Rosemount—Apple Valley—Eagan (Minnesota) School District

Ancient Coins Were Shaped Like Hams

and Other Freaky Facts About Coins, Bills, and Counterfeiting

by **Barbara Seuling**
illustrated by **Matthew Skeens**

PICTURE WINDOW BOOKS
Minneapolis, Minnesota

Editor: Christianne Jones
Designer: Abbey Fitzgerald
Page Production: Melissa Kes
Art Director: Nathan Gassman
The illustrations in this book were created digitally.

Picture Window Books
5115 Excelsior Boulevard
Suite 232
Minneapolis, MN 55416
877-845-8392
www.picturewindowbooks.com

Printed in the United States of America.

All books published by Picture Window Books
are manufactured with paper containing at least
10 percent post-consumer waste.

Library of Congress Cataloging-in-Publication Data
Seuling, Barbara.
Ancient coins were shaped like hams : and other freaky facts
about coins, bills, and counterfeiting / by Barbara Seuling ; illus
trated by Matthew Skeens.
p. cm. — (Freaky facts)
Includes index.
ISBN-13: 978-1-4048-3750-8 (library binding)
ISBN-10: 1-4048-3750-7 (library binding)
1. Money—Juvenile literature. 2. Coins—Juvenile
literature. 3. Paper money—Juvenile literature.
4. Counterfeits and counterfeiting—Juvenile literature.
I. Skeens, Matthew. II. Title.
HG221.5.S477 2007
332.4—dc22   2007004027

Table of Contents

Halfpennies and One-cent Nickels:
Coins

Some ancient coins were shaped like hams.

For a time, China used money that was made of leather.

A Chinese coin from early in the Tang Dynasty (618–907) introduced the practice of inscribing coins. Some people think that a fingernail accidentally made an impression in the wax mold. The impression kept being repeated because no one dared change it.

In 1260 A.D., Louis IX of France had no coins in his treasury to pay his troops. There was no time to mint new coins, so he invented an emergency coin. It was made of a small piece of silver wire snipped off and fastened to a square of leather stamped with its value. These are the coins the troops received for their wages.

Money was once in the form of objects that could be weighed. This explains how the English pound got its name.

Coins were once cut into pieces to make change. That's how Great Britain got its halfpenny and farthings—originally known as "four-things," or fourths of a penny. Similarly, Americans adopted the term "two bits" for a quarter of a dollar. They adopted this from the Spanish dollar, which was divided into eight parts, or bits.

Before the Revolutionary War (1775–1783), the American colonies were desperate for coins. They used any coins that they could get their hands on— French, English, Spanish, and Portuguese.

Henry VIII of England was nicknamed "Old Coppernose" after he issued a poor-quality shilling from which the silver wore off.

The first coins in the American colonies were called "Pine Tree Shillings" for their design. They were produced in Boston in 1652.

The first coin that had the name of the United States of America was the Fugio cent of 1787. It had the motto "Mind Your Business."

A 1792 law directed American money to be made of gold, silver, and copper. Gold was used in the $10, $5, and $2.50 pieces. The dollar, half-dollar, quarter, dime, and half-dime were composed of silver. The cent and half-cent were made of copper.

In 1792, the first official United States Mint was established in Philadelphia. Metals for minting the first coins were scarce. The colonists donated old nails, spikes, finishings from old or wrecked ships, and kitchen utensils. It is said that George Washington donated his wife Martha's "excellent copper teakettle as well as two pairs of tongs" to the cause.

The United States Mint's first gold and silver coins didn't have any numbers on them. People could tell how much coins were worth by their size.

When the first United States Mint was in operation, a citizen could take items that were silver and gold to the Mint to be made into U.S. coins, free of charge.

When the first United States Mint opened, people could visit every day except on Saturdays and rainy days.

The United States' first penny, called the one-cent piece, was almost as big as a half-dollar. It was so big that it was hard to use. However, it wasn't replaced by a smaller penny until 1857.

There was once a one-cent nickel in the United States. In 1857, the large copper cent was changed to a new mix of 87.5 percent copper and 12.5 percent nickel. It was called the nickel cent, which gave way to the nickname "nickel."

The first silver coin in the United States Mint's history to have a value on it was the quarter dollar made in 1804.

The first recorded person to make sure a religious saying deserved to be on U.S. coins was Reverend Watson of Pennsylvania. He wrote to the Secretary of the Treasury, and soon the motto "In God We Trust" appeared on the two-cent coins.

"In God We Trust" was first used on U.S. coins during the Civil War (1861–1865). This inscription was added to the two-cent piece of 1864.

The inclusion of "In God We Trust" on all U.S. currency was required by law in 1955.

From 1875 to 1878, the United States had a coin in the denomination of 20 cents.

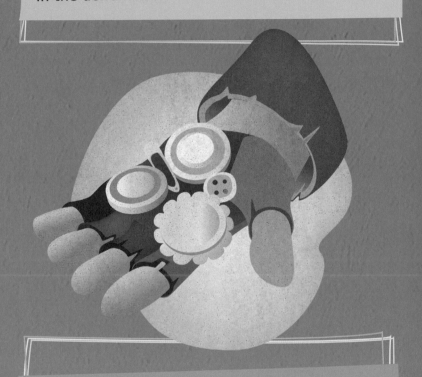

In 1919, after World War I (1914–1918), Germany was bankrupt and manufactured coins from any available materials, including cardboard, glass, porcelain, clay, and cloth. By 1923, the cloth money had been embellished by the addition of lace edgings and fancy needlework.

The buffalo depicted on the 1938 U.S. buffalo nickel was "Black Diamond" from the Bronx Zoo in New York City.

In 1943, a zinc-coated steel penny was produced in the United States so that the more precious metal, copper (which was normally used in pennies), could be used for the war effort.

There's still nickel in the U.S. nickel. The 2006 five-cent coin is the same weight and metal alloy as the original five-cent nickel of 1866.

Once a coin is designed and adopted, it may not be changed for at least 25 years without special legislation.

Fast-paced stamping machines can produce 750 new coins every minute.

In one year, the United States Mint produces between 14 billion and 28 billion circulating coins.

Coins last a lot longer than bills. The life expectancy of a circulating coin is 30 years, while paper money usually only lasts for about 18 months, depending on the denomination of the bill.

Portraits of living people on U.S. coins are extremely rare.

George Washington did not want his portrait on U.S. coins. The symbol of Liberty was used until 1932 when Washington's profile appeared on the quarter.

Nobody knows for sure how the dollar sign came to be. Some say it is the roughly written initials of the country—U.S. Others say that it is a rough form of the figure eight, for the eight-part Spanish dollar on which the U.S. dollar is based. Some people believe that the dollar sign is a modification of the English symbol for the pound: £. The most generally accepted belief is that it is a symbol from the early Phoenicians, signifying strength and sovereignty.

The province of Kweichow, in the Republic of China, produced a silver dollar in 1928. It is probably the only coin in the world that has an automobile as part of its design.

A person who studies coins is called a numismatist.

Some famous coin collectors have included the Roman Emperor Augustus, King George II of England, France's Charlemagne, and Austria's Empress Maria Theresa.

Tree Bark and $2 Bills:
Paper Money

The Bureau of Engraving and Printing produces about 33 million bills a day, which are worth about $529 million. Ninety-five percent of those bills are used to replace bills that can no longer be used.

The pyramid you see on the back of your bills is the reverse side of the Great Seal of the United States. It represents strength and permanence. It has been left unfinished to signify the future growth of the country.

China was the first country to use paper money.

In 1690, the first American paper money was printed by the colony of Massachusetts to pay soldiers.

During the 1600s and 1700s, tobacco was used as money in the Virginia and Maryland colonies.

The paper used in U.S. paper money is specially made by Crane Paper Company of Dalton, Massachusetts. It has been the sole supplier of the special paper since 1879.

The paper used in paper money is 25 percent linen and 75 percent cotton.

It takes about 4,000 double folds (first forward and then backward) before a bill will tear.

The life span of a $1 bill is about 22 months. Then it will likely be too worn to stay in circulation.

The design of paper money is a duty of the U.S. Secretary of the Treasury.

A stack of bills 1 mile (1.6 kilometers) high would contain more than 14.5 million bills.

In 1916, dirty paper money was sent to Washington, D.C., to be laundered. If the money was found to be in good condition, it was washed, ironed, and reissued, saving the U.S. government a few hundred dollars a day in printing costs.

Tree Bark and $2 Bills: Paper Money

By law, no living person can be portrayed on a paper bill of the United States.

Before 1929, U.S. paper money was one-third larger than it is today.

About three hundred $10,000 bills still exist, although they have not been printed by the United States Mint since 1945.

The denominations of U.S. paper money in use today are the $1, $2, $5, $10, $20, $50, and $100 bill.

Counting non-stop at one number per second, it would take you 31 years, 251 days, 7 hours, 46 minutes, and 39 seconds to count $1 billion.

If you had 10 billion $1 bills and spent one every second of every day, it would take 317 years for you to go broke.

Martha Washington is the only woman who has appeared on a U.S. bill. She was on the the $1 Silver Certificate of 1886 and 1891 and on the back of the $1 Silver Certificate of 1896.

It would take 257,588,120 U.S. dollar bills, laid end to end, to circle Earth at the equator.

Following World War II (1939–1945), a Swiss soap manufacturer bought worthless Austrian paper kronen notes and wrapped soap in them.

In 1954, the illusion of the devil's face appeared in the folds of the Queen's hair on a Canadian bank note. No one knows whether the error was an accident or if it was done on purpose.

In India, the one-rupee note has the denomination written out in 18 different dialects, or forms of language.

Since many of their customers could not read, some banks in Wales issued their own private bank notes in the 1700s. The notes had pictures of sheep printed on them.

The world's highest denomination note is the Hungary 100 Million B-Pengo, issued in 1946. That's 100,000,000,000,000,000,000,000 Pengo.

The lowest form of money is the Fiji 1 penny, issued in 1942.

One of the smallest banknotes in the world is the Ivory Coast 0.10 Franc issued in 1920. It is actually a postage stamp pasted on cardboard.

In 1993, a bill with eleven zeros was issued in Yugoslavia. It is the 500,000,000,000 Dinara.

The highest denomination ever printed by the United States is the $100,000 Gold Certificate. They were used only for transactions between the Federal Reserve and the Treasury Department.

The $100 bill has been the largest denomination of U.S. currency in circulation since 1969.

Due to a coin shortage during the Civil War (1861–1865), the Bureau of Engraving and Printing was called upon to print paper notes in denominations of 3 cents, 5 cents, 10 cents, 25 cents, and 50 cents.

The term "buck" came from the Old West, where buckskin was a common item to exchange with Native Americans. Later, as currency replaced the barter system, people referred to a dollar as a buck.

In 1998, to commemorate the Centennial of Independence after more than 300 years of Spanish colonial rule, the government of the Philippines wanted to do something very special. It issued the world's largest banknote.

Fakes and Forgers:
Counterfeiting

Coin clipping was a common practice in medieval times. Coin makers and handlers of large amounts of coins would clip the edges off coins, save up the clippings, and make new coins with them.

Quarters and dimes each have more than 100 ridges around their edges. Without the ridges, it was easy to clip the edges off the coins and save the clippings. The ridges were added to prevent coin clipping.

Sometimes the edges of coins were imprinted with a motto to discourage clipping. One inscription around English coins read: THE PENALTY FOR CLIPPING COINS IS DEATH.

The crime of counterfeiting was taken very seriously in China. Counterfeiters could have had their hands or heads cut off.

Historians believe that Charles IX of France was an excellent counterfeiter. He and his supporters flooded the country with imitation enemy coins in order to force the enemy's economy to decline.

The first currency to be counterfeited in the American colonies was wampum, strings of beads made of shells, which served as money for colonists and native Indians. Colonists and Indians counterfeited some wampum by dying white shells bluish black. The darker-colored shells were more valuable.

There is evidence that counterfeiters have been practicing their craft since about the fourth century B.C.

The practice of transporting criminals to the American colonies was a common English practice. One shipload arrived in Maryland in 1770. Within a few days, counterfeit money had already appeared.

There were several known female counterfeiters in the 13 colonies—two in Connecticut, one in New Hampshire, and seven in Pennsylvania.

To make it more difficult for counterfeiters, South Carolina printed Hebrew letters on its paper money in 1776.

During the French Revolution, the Bank of England, with the approval of the British government, was involved in forgery. The bank created fake French notes.

At a German concentration camp during World War II (1939–1945), several hundred prisoners who were excellent forgers were forced to prepare the plates for counterfeit British pound notes, U.S. dollars, and French franc notes.

In the early 1800s, hundreds of forgers were hanged each year in England.

During the early part of the Civil War (1961–1865), more than one-third of all U.S. currency in circulation was counterfeit. President Abraham Lincoln ordered that a permanent team be set up to stop the counterfeiting problem. The team became the Secret Service.

In its early days, the Secret Service was so diligent that it stopped a Philadelphia baker from baking cookies designed like U.S. pennies.

The U.S. Secret Service doesn't just protect the president. Half of the U.S. Secret Service staff is dedicated to investigating counterfeit currency.

During a severe coin shortage in 1964, many banks and small businesses devised ways to help out. A bank in Wisconsin produced wooden nickels, which local merchants agreed to accept as small change. However, the U.S. Treasury Department forced them to stop because they could have been considered counterfeit.

Counterfeiter J.B. Cross, while serving a term in prison, forged his own pardon from the Governor of Pennsylvania. Only a technicality in how the pardon was presented to prison authorities kept Cross from getting away with it.

Manufacturing counterfeit currency in the United States is punishable by a fine of up to $5,000 or 15 years of imprisonment, or both.

In the United States, about $250,000 in counterfeit money appears every day.

One of the ways the U.S. Federal Reserve detects counterfeit bills is by checking the iron content of the ink.

Curious Customs:
Worldly Money Facts

Every year, natives of the Duke of York Islands in the South Pacific decorate a canoe with green leaves, load it with money, and set it adrift to "pay" the fish for the loss of their relatives that were caught.

The ancient Chinese offered sacrifices regularly to Ts'ai-shen, the god of wealth.

Hard-packed tea leaves pressed into bricks are used as currency in Tibet, Mongolia, and some parts of Siberia.

The ancient Romans considered the god Mercury, known mainly as the runner, as the god of profit.

Coins were once placed on dead bodies, or on their graves, to ensure the deceased would be able to pay the boatman's fare when he or she was ferried over to the land of the dead.

In colonial times, the scarf was a purse worn around the neck.

In the American colonies, only people with more than $200 could wear gold or silver lace or buttons.

It was once a crime punishable by three months' imprisonment for an Englishman who earned less than $20 a year to wear silk in his nightcap.

Chapter Four

The Japanese once used "tree money," which consisted of coins that could be broken down from larger money "branches" to make change.

In India, a cake for a special celebration might be frosted with a thin sheet of real gold, which is eaten along with the cake.

Soap has been used as money in Mexico. It was only valuable if you could still read the name of the town that was stamped on it.

At dances in colonial America, gentlemen danced with ladies in the order of their wealth. The most important male guest danced with the richest girl first, then the second richest, and so on.

The first container that was used for money was probably a money bag, or saccus, according to references in ancient Greek and Roman writings.

Some people used coins to close the eyelids of a corpse. It is believed that the doctor attending President Lincoln at his death placed silver dollars on Lincoln's eyelids.

In China, money started out as symbols of the objects, such as spades and knives, which were once used in trade. Some say that the hole that still appears in the Chinese yen today is leftover from the time when "knife money" had a hole in the handle, probably for stringing the tokens together.

It's a Living:

Jobs and Money

Rembrandt, whose paintings are now valued at millions of dollars each, was poor most of his life. After he died, the Insolvency Office of Amsterdam had to auction all of his possessions in order to pay off his debts.

In medieval times, buying and selling mummies was a profitable business.

In the late 1700s, body snatching was a thriving business. Stolen dead bodies were sold by the shipload to medical schools for anatomical study.

Sigmund Freud's most important work, *The Interpretation of Dreams*, paid the author only $209 when it was published in 1899.

The author of the famous poem "Casey at the Bat," received a payment of only $5 for it.

A private in the Continental Army of the 13 American colonies earned about 52 cents a month.

During his years as a general in the American Revolutionary War, George Washington paid for his own expenses. Congress paid him back after the war. Washington did not want a salary for his service.

Chapter Five

An inventor named Dr. Plimpton earned $1 million for inventing roller skates.

Artist Claude Monet's career began when he won 100,000 francs in the state lottery and became financially independent.

When Thomas Edison learned that his company was making defective batteries in 1905, he paid $1 million of his own money to give refunds.

The famous department store Macy's earned about $11 on its first day of business in 1858.

Artist Andy Warhol said that when he was searching for a subject for his art, a friend asked him what he loved the most. He started painting money.

In 1981, an early self-portrait by artist Pablo Picasso was sold at an auction for $5.3 million.

The president of the United States receives a salary of $400,000 a year. The first president, George Washington, was to receive $25,000 a year. However, Washington refused to accept the salary.

Benjamin Franklin thought the president of the United States should not receive a salary because it would become a corruptive influence.

Glossary

alloy—a substance made by melting and mixing two or more metals with another substance

banknote—a note issued by a bank that is accepted as money

circulation—movement around many different places or from person to person

counterfeiting—making, copying, or imitating something in order to cheat or fool people

currency—the type of money a country uses

denomination—one kind of unit in a system

dialects—different ways of speaking the same language

diligent—working hard and steadily

economy—the way a country produces, distributes, and uses its money, goods, natural resources, and services

embellished—decorated

emperor—a kind of ruler who is like a king

impression—a mark or design produced by pressing or stamping

inscribing—writing, carving, engraving, or marking words or letters on something

laundered—washed

mint—where money is made

natives—people who were born in a particular country or place

note—piece of paper money

numismatist—a person who studies coins

shilling—a coin that was used in Great Britain

sovereignty—supreme excellence

transactions—exchanges of money, goods, or services

Index

39

To Learn More

At the Library

Facklam, Margery, and Margaret Thomas. *The Kids' World Almanac of Amazing Facts About Numbers, Math, and Money*. New York: World Almanac, 1992.

Parker, Nancy Winslow. *Money, Money, Money: The Meaning of the Art and Symbols on United States Paper Currency*. New York: HarperCollins Publishers, 1995.

On the Web

FactHound offers a safe, fun way to find Web sites related to this book. All of the sites on FactHound have been researched by our staff.

1. Visit *www.facthound.com*
2. Type in this special code: 1404837507
3. Click on the FETCH IT button.

Your trusty FactHound will fetch the best sites for you!

Look for all of the books in the Freaky Facts series:

Ancient Coins Were Shaped Like Hams and Other Freaky Facts About Coins, Bills, and Counterfeiting

Cows Sweat Through Their Noses and Other Freaky Facts About Animal Habits, Characteristics, and Homes

Earth Is Like a Giant Magnet and Other Freaky Facts About Planets, Oceans, and Volcanoes

Three Presidents Died on the Fourth of July and Other Freaky Facts About the First 25 Presidents

Your Skin Weighs More Than Your Brain and Other Freaky Facts About Your Skin, Skeleton, and Other Body Parts